GET UP!

A 30-DAY
DEVOTIONAL

Dr. Stacia K. Wilkins

ISBN 978-1-0980-7036-6 (paperback)
ISBN 978-1-0980-7037-3 (digital)

Christian Faith Publishing, Inc.
832 Park Avenue
Meadville, PA 16335
www.christianfaithpublishing.com

Printed in the United States of America

CONTENTS

ACKNOWLEDGMENTS

I would like to thank all my amazing family and friends for your constant support throughout my life and this project. A special shout-out to my parents, Kenneth Hooper and Vanessa Hooper, for always letting me know that I can. Thank you to Christian Faith Publishing for making this a pleasurable and seamless process. Thank you to Kevin Johnson for designing the book cover at the 11th hour—your gifts and talents are unparalleled bro! My husband, Andre Wilkins, you are truly my ordinary extraordinary. Without your idea, creativity, and encouragement, this book would not have been written. Thank you for your selfless love toward me and your selfless sharing of me with the world. I dedicate this book to you. Lastly, to my Lord and Savior, Jesus Christ, You are the resurrection and the life. I'm able to live out my name because You've lived out Yours. My heart belongs to You forever.

INTRODUCTION
THE SERMON THAT CHANGED
MY LIFE

In August of 2018, I was invited to preach at a women's conference in Philadelphia, Pennsylvania. If I remember correctly, the theme of the conference was "Arise." So in normal "preacher fashion," I went before God in prayer to seek Him about what He would have me to say to these women. My thought was, this should be an easy sermon to prepare because there's so much the Bible had to say about that. However, I found myself caught between two texts in particular: the account of Lazarus and the account of Jairus' daughter. I kept feeling drawn to the story of Jairus' daughter and soon realized this was the message God wanted me to minister at the conference. Little did I know, this would be more than a one-time sermon. It would, in fact, be my personal life's message and a continued journey.

Following my delivery of the sermon, I reflected as I often do and realized that this time felt different. This was the first time I felt I had entered into who I fully was as a minister and as a woman. For the first time, I felt I had merged with the woman I would often see in my dreams. It was almost like it was a spiritual coming-of-age experience for me. Not just that, but I also saw how God moved mightily in the service: the altar was full. It was one of the most powerful moments I had experienced in my life. I was eternally grateful. But something changed afterward. I wasn't the same. I felt my whole life shift. Weeks and months went by, and I realized I couldn't shake this sermon off of me. This Word stayed with me and fastened itself to me and wouldn't let me go. I shared this with my husband, and he told me that maybe God was trying to speak to me about this being more than a sermon. He went on to say, "Maybe He wants to take you on a deeper journey. Maybe you should do like a 30-day devotional and see what He gives you each day." Though he casually mentioned this, a light bulb went off in my head. I ran to my prayer room and asked God what he wanted me to do about this. He confirmed what my husband said! This is why it's important to have a priest in the home who can speak into your life on multiple levels because he understands and supports where you're going in God and in life (that's a plug for the single ladies). Okay, so I digress. Back to the story!

So I went and bought a notebook and began this 30-day journey with prayer. Daily, God would give me insights into the full account of Jairus' daughter in Matthew 5 as He walked me through my own journey. In all transparency, I didn't complete this in 30 days. Inconsistency, emotional struggles, a doctoral dissertation, life, laziness, fear, and, at times, a lack of submission all contributed to my prolonged journey. There were times when I abandoned my devotion and allowed these other things to get in the way. Furthermore, I knew that I would have to walk all of these things out and be without excuse, which I wasn't totally ready for. However, God has a way of making all things work together for good.

I implore you to make this an intentional read. This book is not designed for you to read straight through page by page. Instead, it's to slow you down so you can reflect daily on where you currently are in your life and where you are with God. For each day, you will find a topic that pertains to the scriptural account of Jairus' daughter, a relatable story, an application, a prayer that you can pray, and a reflection question for you to ponder and answer.

It is my prayer that you will allow this to be an intimate journey between you and Christ and that in this journey, you will rediscover who you are. I pray that He will comfort the painful and uncomfortable areas you will face while on this journey. I pray that your faith won't fail and that you will stick with it whether it takes you 30 days or longer. I pray that you will take back your power as you understand the resurrection power that lives within you. I pray that everything connected to you will grow from a dry state to a fruitful state. Take one day at a time and listen to what God is speaking to you. Let's get up together!

While He was still speaking, some came from the ruler of the synagogue's house who said, "Your daughter is dead. Why trouble the Teacher any further?" As soon as Jesus heard the word that was spoken, He said to the ruler of the synagogue, "Do not be afraid; only believe." And He permitted no one to follow Him except Peter, James, and John the brother of James. Then He came to the house of the ruler of the synagogue, and saw a tumult and those who wept and wailed loudly. When He came in, He said to them, "Why make this commotion and weep? The child is not dead, but sleeping." And they ridiculed Him. But when He had put them all outside, He took the father and the mother of the child, and those who were with Him, and entered where the child was lying. Then He took the child by the hand, and said to her, "Talitha, cumi," which is translated, "Little girl, I say to you, arise." Immediately the girl arose and walked, for she was twelve years of age. And they were overcome with great amazement. But He commanded them strictly that no one should know it, and said that something should be given her to eat.
—Mark 5:35–43 (NKJV)

DAY

Location

Location, location, location! When considering the purchase of a home, realtors have typically encouraged homebuyers to consider three things: location, location, location! This became a traditional real estate mantra around 1952. Location for a home was important because it needed to be within walking distance of shopping centers and community stores. There needed to be rapid transportation access to the nearest city and offices via highways, and it needed to be convenient to places of worship, hospitals, and schools.

So when we meet Jairus' daughter in the text, one of the most obvious highlights is her location. She was located in a house likely in the city of Capernaum, which is situated on the Sea of Galilee. This city is close to community outlets, transportation via the Sea of Galilee, and is close to a synagogue. Capernaum was a dwelling city for Jesus. It was a place where He frequented; it was His home. Capernaum was the place of many of Jesus' miracles. Regardless of what was happening in this city, Jesus was present.

Wherever you are now, know that Jesus is present. He's right there with you. Though it may not seem like it, He is in the same city, state, country, and continent you're in. Jesus is fully capable of navigating through geography to be closer to you. But the question is, do you want Him to come? All He needs is an invitation.

Prayer

God, I pray for Your visitation and Your presence. I invite You to find me at my physical location today. I'll wait for You to come and make Yourself known to me. In Jesus' name, amen.

Reflection Question

Where are you right now, and what is preventing you from inviting God in?

_____

_____

_____

_____

_____

_____

_____

_____

_____

_____

_____

_____

_____

_____

_____

_____

_____

_____

_____

_____

_____

DAY

2

Setting

In a novel or a movie, the setting is probably the most important element of a story next to the plot. Whereas the location points to a physical geographical area, the setting refers to the context for which the story is set. The setting is the timing of the story, the climate, and the circumstances surrounding it. The story of the damsel (Jairus' daughter) is found in the context of healing. We see this in the preceding verses where Jesus cast out the demons of the man who lived among the tombs, healed the woman with the issue of blood, and other miraculous occurrences. Amid so much sickness and chaos, Jesus was there to bring one thing to the atmosphere: healing.

It's funny how the city of Capernaum was known as a city of comfort, yet there was so much distress. Jesus entered into a city that was living the opposite of its name. He had to *be* the comfort (the healing) it needed to be restored to its proper condition. That's what He wants to do with us. He wants to bring healing to your atmosphere. The timing is now. It's time to heal.

Prayer

Lord, please help me to recognize the timing in my life and that I am purposed for healing. Flood my atmosphere now with Your healing. I petition Your healing balm to find me exactly where I am. In Jesus' name, amen.

Reflection Question

What has happened to you?

_____

_____

_____

_____

_____

_____

_____

_____

_____

_____

_____

_____

_____

_____

_____

_____

_____

_____

_____

_____

_____

_____

DAY

3

Something Is Wrong

Ever say that to yourself, "Something is wrong"? You haven't quite put your finger on it or figure out exactly what is wrong, but you do know something isn't right. It's almost like you're coming down with a cold or something, and you're not sure what it is, but you know your body isn't feeling right. I can only imagine that this is probably how Jairus' daughter began to feel before her sickness progressed.

The interesting thing about an infection or a virus is that it is usually present in the body days before symptoms appear. When it multiplies and the cells within our body are damaged as a result of the infection, a disease has developed. Primary and secondary prevention teach us the necessity of treating something potentially damaging before it has developed and even as it is developing. It is important for us to pay attention to our bodies because they function as powerful sources of information.

We also must pay close attention to our souls and spirits. What are our souls and spirits trying to tell us? Do you feel distant from God? Are you feeling sad, depressed, angry, bored, lonely, or undervalued? If so, something must be wrong. It's up to you to find out what's really going on.

Prayer

God, please show me, *me*. Things have been feeling a little off lately. I need Your insights to see. Please reveal the infection that has taken up residence in me. In Jesus' name, amen.

Reflection Question

In what ways have you not been feeling like yourself?

_____

_____

_____

_____

_____

_____

_____

_____

_____

_____

_____

_____

_____

_____

_____

_____

_____

DAY

4

Sickness Gone Wild

Full-blown sickness and feeling helpless—I can only imagine the pain and agony Jairus' daughter must've been in. It's almost like suddenly something hit her body and crippled her to the point where it became evident that she needed help. I'm sure the signs and symptoms were already there. Maybe no one took it seriously and thought she'd be okay. Perhaps even she concealed the pain, or maybe she had been here before and thought she'd come out of it just like the last time. Who knows! Whatever the case, the sickness was rapidly progressing, and she wasn't getting better.

Perhaps some of the signs and symptoms have been there for you to indicate that sickness has come upon you. Maybe you have been feeling actual pain in your body. Maybe you are feeling overwhelmingly hopeless, deeply jealous, insecure, or ardently angry. Whatever illness has befallen you, it's time to acknowledge it so it can be treated. Otherwise, you may infect or contaminate others.

Prayer

God, I'm not feeling well today, and I haven't been for a while now. I must admit that I'm sick, and if I'm honest, it feels like it's overtaking me. I'm asking You to reveal to me what this sickness is because I desire to be made whole. Help me! In Jesus' name, amen.

Reflection Question

What infection has taken residence in you (i.e., anger, jealousy, stress, etc)?

_____

_____

_____

_____

_____

_____

_____

_____

_____

_____

_____

_____

_____

_____

_____

_____

_____

_____

_____

DAY

5

A Concerned Father

There's something to be said about the care, compassion, and urgency of a parent when a child falls ill. Growing up, I remember my parents immediately coming to my aid whenever I got sick. One of the things I distinctly remember is the concern I saw in their eyes. I'm certain that it was the concern that drove them to do everything in their power to help me get better. I'm sure there was no difference with Jairus. Though he was a synagogue leader, Jairus was first a concerned father who wanted his daughter to be well. The difference, however, between Jairus and my parents in the moment of sickness is that Jairus realized that there was nothing else he could do. His daughter wasn't showing signs of improvement. She was in fact dying. In a moment of desperation, the only thing left for Jairus to do was go find Jesus, and he did.

When everything is falling apart and you see no improvement, there is someone you can go to. Jairus taught us a valuable lesson here because in the face of his turmoil, he remembered Jesus. The Bible says he fell at Jesus' feet and begged Jesus to lay His hands on his daughter so she would be healed (verses 22 and 23). Jairus was able to demonstrate a type of intercession on behalf of his daughter. So whatever state you find yourself in, remember, there is someone concerned about you. Whether you're reading this book in a hospital bed, in your bedroom, on your job, or in front of a bottle of pills that you're about to take to end your life, know that someone is interceding for you. Whether you have parents, family, or none, Jesus

Himself makes the intercession for you before the Father (Romans 8:34, Hebrews 7:25).

Prayer

Lord, when I can't pray for myself, You can. When I don't have the words to describe what I feel, You understand. You know the way to the Father. Pray for me. You know the people who love me and are concerned about me. Move upon their hearts to pray for me. You are a good, good Father, and I thank You for praying for me. In Jesus' name, amen.

Reflection Question

How do you feel about your father, and how has this affected the way you view God?

_____

_____

_____

_____

_____

_____

_____

_____

_____

_____

_____

_____

_____

_____

_____

_____

_____

_____

DAY

6

She's Dead

There's nothing like hearing the news that someone you know and love has died. There is a wave of sadness, shock, unbelief, anger, and helplessness that runs through your body upon receipt of the news. Death seems to bring with it such finality because everything you once knew about the person is gone. The only thing left is the memory. Jairus must've completely been beside himself when he found out his daughter was gone. I can only imagine the helplessness and irritation he felt when he was told to not even bother to get Jesus to help since his daughter was already dead. Though he felt helpless, it seemed like he was not hopeless. For some reason, he still believed in her life.

Ever witness yourself dying or die? Yes, that feeling when the cares of this life completely overtake you and your soul becomes entangled in a web of lifelessness. When you've stopped praying, stopped reading the Bible, and every part of your body just becomes still, you've resigned yourself to believe that this is just how it's going to be, and there's nothing you can do about it. I know the feeling. I also know the truth. I know a Man who is the resurrection and the life! Jairus knew Him too. His name is Jesus, and He's on His way.

Prayer

Lord, something in me has died. Maybe I have died. My passions are gone, every day is just another day, and I don't have the strength to continue. I don't know what else to do. So out of desperation, I'll just call on Your name, *Jesus, Jesus, Jesus!* Your name is my prayer. Amen.

Reflection Question

What has died in you?

_____

_____

_____

_____

_____

_____

_____

_____

_____

_____

_____

_____

_____

_____

_____

_____

_____

_____

_____

_____

DAY

7

Someone Is Coming

It's always good to know when assistance is on the way, especially when something overwhelming, traumatic, or undesirable has happened. When you know that someone who is skilled to help you and who brings you to a place of recovery is on the way, your spirit gains strength. That's when you're alive. But there's no voice and hope in the grave. When death has occurred, the dead person cannot speak for himself/herself. But thank God for the Advocate who can speak for us!

No matter where you find yourself, know that there's the Advocate who speaks on your behalf. He's coming to see about you because someone cares enough to go to Him on your behalf. He knows exactly where you are. He knows just what's going on with you. He is willing to come, and He is fully confident in His ability to bring you back to life. He's ready and en route to you. He's coming!

Prayer

Lord, even when I can't say the words, You know exactly where I am. You know precisely what I need. I believe it's time for resuscitation. Come, Lord Jesus! Amen.

Reflection Question

Who and what does your support system consist of, and how do you feel supported?

_____

_____

_____

_____

_____

_____

_____

_____

_____

_____

_____

_____

_____

_____

_____

_____

_____

_____

DAY

8

Delay

I absolutely *love* shoes! One of the most exciting things (other than ordering and receiving them) is tracking their route to me. There's such anticipation that comes with knowing they're on the way. However, I have found myself to become completely annoyed when I see that the package has been delayed due to a storm, holiday, or any other reason. My irritation comes from two main things: (1) the fact that they are supposed to be here by a certain time and (2) my concern about whether or not they will actually get to me.

The cliché "delay is not denial" has been so overly stated. Let's be honest: Who actually wants to hear that? Healing was on the way to Jairus' daughter, but Jesus had some other stops to make along the way. I'm sure Jairus had to realize that it wasn't just about him and what he needed. And we have to understand this as well. So I'll just say, you haven't been forgotten. Jesus is still on His way to you. There will come a time in His journey that He'll make a beeline straight to your house, steps uninterrupted. Sometimes our urgency is the reason for His delay.

Prayer

God, You must see the state that I'm in. If You don't get here soon, it's gonna be it for me. Please give me grace for the delay. In Jesus' name, amen.

Reflection Question

What bothers you the most about something being delayed?

_____

_____

_____

_____

_____

_____

_____

_____

_____

_____

_____

_____

_____

_____

_____

_____

_____

_____

_____

_____

_____

_____

DAY

9

Don't Fear, Just Believe

Life circumstances have a way of causing a major disruption in our emotional equilibrium. This, in turn, can produce extreme levels of anxiety and fear while threatening the very core of our belief system that we once trusted in. As soon as Jesus heard that the girl was now dead, He immediately turned to Jairus and said, "Do not be afraid. Only believe." It was almost as if Jesus sensed what Jairus was feeling in real time. And before his emotions had the chance to completely take over him, Jesus spoke a word. In essence, He told Jairus not to get caught up in what was happening but look forward to something more promising, even if there was no physical evidence for it. Essentially, Jesus was telling Jairus to have faith.

What happened to your faith? What happened to the times when you would believe everything God told you as if you were a child? The enemy has crept into our belief systems and used the power of suggestion to cause us to consider something other than what God has said. No matter what has happened, it's not too late to revive your faith. Fear has no power when you just believe.

Prayer

Lord, I'm afraid of what I don't know. How can I not believe what's before my eyes? Please help my unbelief so even in this, I can fully trust that You are going to come through for me. In Jesus' name, amen.

Reflection Question

In which areas of your life have you stopped believing and become more fearful?

_____

_____

_____

_____

_____

_____

_____

_____

_____

_____

_____

_____

_____

_____

_____

_____

_____

_____

DAY

10

And The Band Played On

No, I'm not talking about the movie *And the Band Played On* with Tom Hanks and Denzel Washington. Instead, I am referring to the meaning of the expression. "And the band played on" is a creative way of saying, "Business as usual." And isn't that what we find once Jesus arrived at the house where Jairus' daughter was? Professional mourners, wailers, and instrumentalists were there to greet Him upon His arrival. Jesus walked into a situation where people were basically saying, "What are you here for? This is our routine when things like this happen." In a way, they would be right because when someone died back in those days, they actually had professional mourners and instrumentalists come to the home to begin the funeral process. But Jesus was coming to disturb their groove. He brought disruption to their melancholy.

I believe Jesus is coming to interrupt your "business as usual." No more continuing through things apart from Him. Will you try to continue your "business as usual" right in His face? What has happened in your life that has become such a part of your adopted routine yet it is no longer serving you?

Prayer

Lord, I invite You to come and disturb the faulty routines that do not serve me or honor You. I don't want to continue in "business as usual" when You've taken the time to grace me with Your presence. In Jesus' name, amen.

Reflection Question

How do you handle life or your normal routines being interrupted?

_____

_____

_____

_____

_____

_____

_____

_____

_____

_____

_____

_____

_____

_____

_____

_____

_____

_____

_____

DAY

11

Why The Fuss?

Ever walk down the street and you hear yelling or other kinds of disturbing sounds? It makes you curious about what is actually going on. What's all the fuss about? Who's involved? Why is everyone here? It's really a whole dramatic scene that is evoking so many different emotions. Some of those emotions are sadness, anger, surprise, and even disbelief about what's going on. There's so much noise.

This is what Jesus walked into when He arrived at Jairus' home: a bunch of noise. People were wailing, crying, talking, and playing instruments all because a girl had died. I can only imagine how loud and chaotic this really was and, quite frankly, how annoying this must've been. It even provoked Jesus to ask them why they were making all this commotion and tumult. In essence, He was saying, "Why are you making all this noise and causing all this confusion?" And, especially, why were they doing all of this upon His arrival?

It's so interesting how our lives and our minds become so noisy because of what's going on. We react so much to external circumstances and ultimately cause ourselves so much turmoil and confusion. Perhaps we should begin to train our minds and our mouths to stop the chatter when Christ makes His presence known in our specific situations. Why are you fussing? He's here. Be still.

Prayer

Lord, please forgive me for all of the chatter that goes on in my mind and comes out of my mouth. I repent of the thoughts and words flowing from me that refuse to yield to you. Help me to start focusing more on You and stop fussing about what I believe has taken place. In Jesus' name, amen.

Reflection Question

What are the thoughts that are constantly flowing through your mind? In what ways has your life become too noisy?

_____

_____

_____

_____

_____

_____

_____

_____

_____

_____

_____

_____

_____

_____

_____

_____

_____

_____

_____

DAY

12

It's Not What It Looks Like

It's crazy how all the signs can point to one reality, yet what's really going on is the opposite reality. I'm reminded of the saying, "You think you know, but you have no idea." Things are not always what they seem. There is often a deeper reality than what appears on the surface.

After all of the tears, confusion, anxiety, and commotion that was going on, it turned out that what they thought happened to the girl really didn't happen. Jesus said that the girl everyone thought was dead was actually sleeping. She looked dead, but she was actually alive! She was just in a dormant state. But Jesus gave her a prognosis. In her "dead" state, His report said that she would live.

What is lying dormant in you? What is it about you that you have given up because of how things look? I submit to you that your reality may be far from the truth. God is about to reveal your prognosis. Whose report will you believe?

Prayer

Lord, things look pretty dim. Help me to accept Your word against my own. My perception has deceived me. What You say is what shall be. In Jesus' name, amen.

Reflection Question

What is lying dormant in you?

_____

_____

_____

_____

_____

_____

_____

_____

_____

_____

_____

_____

_____

_____

_____

_____

_____

_____

_____

_____

DAY

13

Mockery

As a young girl and well into my teenage years, I was often made fun of, talked about, and laughed at. I remember my parents always telling me to ignore the people who did that to me, but it was really difficult to do that when they were always in my face. It affected me deeply and well into my adulthood. The residual effects of that rejection sometimes still affect me today. However, as I matured, I learned that people often make fun of and talk nasty about the people they don't understand and/or people who are different from them. When I learned this, I was able to embrace my uniqueness much more and be comfortable in my own skin.

This is what I love about Jesus in this story. He was completely comfortable in His own skin. He was perfectly fine being all that He was and doing whatever He knew He needed to do, even if people mocked Him. In the story, it says that the people outside laughed at Him to scorn when He arrived at the house. But He threw them out! Ha! That was funny to me! He recognized who He needed with Him and who He didn't. Whatever the people said, it didn't stop Him from what He knew He had to do.

Have you shut down your dreams, your vision, and your purpose because the people laughed at it? Have you muted yourself in hopes that you won't be noticed? Sometimes we react within instead of reacting outwardly. We internalize what the people do to us and allow it to alter who we are. Jesus didn't do that. He continued to be Himself amid the laughs and the mockery. If we are to look at this in modern terms, it's as if Jesus was saying, "Oh, okay, y'all can stay out here and laugh if you want to. But I got a girl to heal, so move out of My way!" The moral of the story here is, don't allow anyone to dummy down who you are!

Prayer

Lord, words hurt, but Your words heal. Help me to believe what You've always said about me, and help me to discover the parts of me that I haven't heard You mention just yet. In Jesus' name, amen.

Reflection Question

In what ways have you stopped being you or proceeding with your plan because of the mockery of others?

_____

_____

_____

_____

_____

_____

_____

_____

_____

_____

_____

_____

_____

_____

_____

_____

_____

DAY

14

Good Company

Ever go somewhere and there are only certain people whom you'll take to a particular place? There are specific reasons why you take these people. Sometimes those are the people you'll have the most fun with, they are the most relatable, or they'll typically have your back if something goes wrong. Whatever the reason, those people accompany you for a specific purpose you are trying to fulfill.

Jesus had now arrived at the house, and He's ready to raise this girl back to life. But He didn't come alone. He brought with Him Peter, James, and John, His most beloved disciples. Not only did He trust them to witness what He was about to do, but He also had to train them to do this same work. Jesus also invited the parents to come into where the girl lay not just because they were connected to her but also because of their faith in His ability.

It's time to check your circle and your covenant relationships. Everyone can't go with you because everyone is not prepared. God will send those who will help you get the job done. Don't worry, you won't go alone.

Prayer

Lord, please show me who is really for me and who is for Your purpose. Please surround me with those who will help me rise. In Jesus' name, amen.

Reflection Question

Who are your covenant relationships with, and in what ways do they hold you accountable and help you grow?

_____

_____

_____

_____

_____

_____

_____

_____

_____

_____

_____

_____

_____

_____

_____

_____

_____

_____

DAY

15

Lying Down

I can't tell you how many times I hit the snooze button every morning when my alarm goes off. Even though I know it's time for me to begin getting ready for my workday, I just don't feel like getting out of bed yet. I usually convince myself that five or ten more minutes will make a difference in my readiness, so I keep lying there. Why? Because I'm comfortable where I am. I've been lying down for a good six to eight hours, and I'm not ready to get up. Yet something has changed. It seems like my internal alarm clock keeps going off, and it won't cease until I actually get up.

Jairus' daughter was found lying down. She had been in one position for some time. She was forced to lie down because of her sickness. But Jesus saw fit for her to no longer lie down. In His eyes, that wasn't where she belonged. The time had come for her to change positions.

Why are you lying down? What has forced you to be immobile? After you have slept for a few hours, your brain signals your body to awaken and resume activity. It's a biological fact! As it is in the natural, so it is in the spiritual. Whether you've been in a restful period, a depressed period, or an unmotivated period, Jesus has come to change your state. Lying there, lifeless, is no longer an option for you.

Prayer

Lord, I have admittedly become comfortable lying down, but something in me is awakening. Help the rest of me get into alignment. In Jesus' name, amen.

Reflection Question

In what areas of your life have you become complacent?

_____

_____

_____

_____

_____

_____

_____

_____

_____

_____

_____

_____

_____

_____

_____

_____

_____

_____

_____

THE TRANSITION
PART 1

In all integrity, I must admit that I took a break on this journey and couldn't figure out why. I completely stopped writing. It happened right after Day 15 when I talked about lying down. Interesting, huh? I felt like I was in between two places, and I had come to a critical point: Do I stay, or do I grow? For me, staying became increasingly comfortable, lustfully complacent, and self-soothing. It seemed to be serving me well. Yet when I would go back in prayer before God, there was a glaring reality that my comfort was not serving Him. In fact, it was unyielding, unaccountable, and it was enmity toward Him. I didn't want to be in direct opposition with God, and I knew that my comfort was 100 percent beneficial toward me. I was being completely selfish and had to determine who and what I was going to choose. I knew it was time to change postures, but I did not want to do the work required to change postures.

God has a way of using everyday circumstances to bring revelatory knowledge to us. During this time, I was working with a personal trainer at a gym, and he had me doing floor exercises one day. When I finished the exercises, I was just lying on the floor because I felt like I could not use my ab, arm, or leg muscles to push myself up. I was extremely tired from the workout, so I just lay there. The trainer then shouted, "Come on, get up!" Without hesitation, I replied, "I can't." What he did next completely changed the moment. He simply reached out his hand for me to grab and said, "Come on, I got you." I remember lying there, looking at his hand, and thinking, "Oh, is he serious? Like, he's really not gonna let me lie here?" I had to make a quick decision because I realized I was no longer on my time; I was on his time. So I reached up and grabbed his hand, mustered whatever strength I didn't know I had in my muscles, sat up, and pushed myself off the floor while he pulled me up the rest of the way. I would later realize that my personal trainer and I literally partnered to get me from one place (posture) to the next.

God showed me that this is what He's trying to do. God wants to partner with me, and He wants to partner with you to get to that next place. See, I was afraid to be "her." I didn't know how to be "her"—her being the woman that I've always felt and seen in my dreams. It's uncomfortable being her, even though being her is being a better, more committed, and healthier me. God is trying to take you out of your low places to experience the height and depth of who He is. Only then will you truly understand yourself. Yes, it requires work, some accountability, and consistency on our part, but He'll pull you up the rest of the way. He's ready to partner with you in this transition. You have reached the point of no return. The remainder of this book will be you operating in a different posture, living in a resurrected state. God's got you! Will you take His hand?

DAY

16

His Hand

Biblically speaking, the hand has often been a symbol of human action and divine power. In other words, there is a human movement that takes place and a simultaneous divine exchange. Notice in the text, Jesus took Jairus' daughter's hand, meaning He put His hand onto her hand. Interestingly, He did not lay hands on her forehead or any other part of her body. Nor did He use His hands to completely pick her up from where she lay. He simply just took her hand. Essentially, He connected His power with her power and His ability with her ability. I can only imagine how great that power surge was between them at that very moment. They connected so she could be resurrected.

Perhaps it's been a while since you've really connected with God. Now is the time. He has taken the initiative to place His hand onto your hand because He's ready for something powerful to happen. Are you ready? The power surge has come!

Prayer

Lord, thank You for taking the initiative to reach out to me. I've allowed so many minor and major things to consume me to the point that I disconnected from You. I'm ready to plug back in now. Send Your power! Endow me once again. In Jesus' name, amen.

Reflection Question

What has stripped you of your power and abilities?

_____

_____

_____

_____

_____

_____

_____

_____

_____

_____

_____

_____

_____

_____

_____

_____

_____

_____

_____

_____

_____

DAY

17

Arise

Jesus simply said, "*Talitha, cumi,*" to the little girl, which is easily translated as "Damsel (little girl), arise!" In our modern-day vernacular, it says, "Get up!" This was the moment of complete transition, the moment when death shifted to life and when immobility shifted to mobility. This was the moment that people had been waiting for, for this little girl—a complete recovery, a complete return back to life. At this moment, it did not matter what happened to her before. All that mattered was that Jesus was present, and He alone had the power to heal and resurrect her. His two words had the power and the authority to bring her back from the grave. His words have that same authority in your life.

The truth is, God wants us to live! The only thing on us or in us that should be dead is sin. We are expected to live out His commands. So wherever you are in your life, He is telling you to arise! It's time to get up! No more lying down, no more lifelessness, and no more hopelessness. It's time now. You have much to do! Get up!

Prayer

Lord, it's been a struggle, and this sickness has me down for some time. But now, I have no excuse because You have commanded me to arise. Help me now to shift upward. Raise me up! In Jesus' name, amen.

Reflection Question

What does getting up look like for you?

_____

_____

_____

_____

_____

_____

_____

_____

_____

_____

_____

_____

_____

_____

_____

_____

_____

_____

_____

_____

DAY

18

Listening

In Hebrews 3:15, it says that if we hear His voice, we are not to harden our hearts. One remarkable thing about this little girl was that even in a dead state, she heard the voice of God. She gave ear to Jesus telling her to arise. There was no wall erected in her heart against His word that would prevent it from penetrating her spirit. Clearly, she wasn't even hardened by how she got in that sick and dead position in the first place. When all else was silent, she heard Jesus' voice. This is so clear because in order to respond, one must first listen. His voice was powerful enough to reach her beyond this natural world and call her back from death.

The Lord has already told you to arise. Are you listening? Break down the walls and the barriers that have caused you to reject His voice. Because we are His creations, we must respond to Him. We must listen to do the very thing we were created to do. Harden not your hearts. Listen! Get up!

Prayer

God, break down every part of me that will not yield to Your voice. I desire to hear You clearly. Speak, Lord. In Jesus' name, amen.

Reflection Question

What are the walls in your life or your heart that prevent you from hearing God's voice and acting on what He says?

_____

_____

_____

_____

_____

_____

_____

_____

_____

_____

_____

_____

_____

_____

_____

_____

_____

_____

DAY

19

Obedience

The Bible has much to say about obedience. The very act of obedience is of the utmost importance to God. In fact, in John 14, Jesus said that if we love Him, we'll keep His commandments. This tells me that obedience carries a cognitive component as well as a behavioral component. We are to be decisive about obedience, and we are to model an expression of obedience. Jairus' daughter exemplified this perfectly. When Jesus spoke, she responded to what He said by doing exactly what He told her to do. The Bible admonishes us to not just be hearers of the Word and deceive ourselves but to also do what it says. Jesus spoke a word to her to arise, and she did just that. She came out of her slumbered state and rose to life. She became what He said to her—she became a risen daughter.

What has God spoken to you? Have you ignored it? Did you just hear it and did nothing about it? Did you think what He said was for another day? He says for us to arise, and His word requires your response! His word cannot return to Him void. It's time to be obedient to your resurrection. Get up!

Prayer

Lord, please help me to be a doer of Your Word. With Your mighty power, break every mental, emotional, physical, spiritual, or relational chain that keeps me from living an obedient life. Help me to rise to the occasion at the command of Your Word to live a fully resurrected life. In Jesus' name, amen.

Reflection Question

What has God been speaking to you about you, your life, and the next steps? Why have you been hardheaded (stubborn)?

_____

_____

_____

_____

_____

_____

_____

_____

_____

_____

_____

_____

_____

_____

_____

_____

_____

_____

_____

_____

_____

DAY

20

Repositioning

Today, I woke up and was excited that I didn't have anything to do until the afternoon. Because I didn't have any plans, I said to myself that I could go back to sleep. I actually became frustrated when I realized I could not fall back to sleep. I was in a completely awakened state, even though I wanted to continue to lie down. This really spoke to me about repositioning. No matter what you feel like and no matter what you want to do, things change when you have been repositioned, and you won't be able to return to your previous state of inactivity or stagnation. Jairus' daughter was repositioned in response to Jesus telling her to arise. She went from lying down to sitting up, from unconsciousness to awareness, and from inaction to action. She entered into a different state of being.

May I now say to you, "Welcome to your repositioning!" You have entered into a new posture, one that's upright and full of purpose and one that is literally designed to propel you into the greatest version of yourself. It is time to be your resurrected self, live your resurrected dream, and to be a force of resurrection to a dying world. You carry *the resurrection* within you! Our bodies are the temples of the Holy Spirit. You have the resurrection power because you are a carrier of the resurrection! Get up!

Prayer

Lord, I thank You for the repositioning that is greater than my feelings, greater than my doubts, and greater than me. Please help me to remain in the right position. In Jesus' name, amen.

Reflection Question

How does it feel to be repositioned and no longer in a rut?

_____

_____

_____

_____

_____

_____

_____

_____

_____

_____

_____

_____

_____

_____

_____

_____

_____

_____

_____

_____

THE TRANSITION PART 2

Admittedly, I ended up taking another break during this process right after Day 20 when I talked about repositioning. This break was actually longer than the first one—more like a hiatus. I guess I didn't realize how jarring repositioning could really be. Sometimes it is not as kind, not as exciting, and not as comforting as we imagine it to be. It simply just is another moment of stagnation, sitting up but still can't get going and standing up while surveying all of your surroundings with each of your senses and still not walking forward. You realize it's a new space, a new atmosphere, and a new day that's very unfamiliar yet highly stimulating all at the same time. Whoa! What is all of this?

This is exactly what happened to me once I finished my doctorate. Three weeks later, my grandmother passed away. People were pulling on me from different areas. I still had to work. A whole lot of other things were happening. I was utterly exhausted yet couldn't lie back down because I had been repositioned. I needed time to gather myself.

Have you ever been sitting down for so long and when you try to get up, you feel a bit dizzy for a few seconds? So you need time to get yourself together. Sometimes you may need to hold onto something for a little while just to get your balance back or at least until the room stops spinning. I can only imagine how Jairus' daughter must've felt being jolted from death back into life, being jolted from a sleep state to a state of alertness. Think about the surge that must've gone through every part of her biological, psychological, and spiritual systems all at once when Jesus spoke to her and she was swiftly repositioned. What happened to her was immediate, intentional, and unapologetic albeit overwhelming. Yet she couldn't go back to being dead, and she could not return to her previous posture.

God has a way of transporting us without our permission yet for His mission, and sometimes we are left to figure things out. We then question, Where am I, what happened to me, who am I in this place? Amid this curiosity, uncertainty, fear, and even frustration, God does not reverse His command. So as you've been repositioned, you may need to take some time to gather yourself and make a new assessment because after this, there's only movement!

Prayer

Lord, thank You for Your mercy in giving me time to gather myself. Help me to move forward now in Your vision for my life. In Jesus' name, amen.

DAY

21

Walk

When I woke up this morning, I remember sitting up and then swinging my legs over the bed preparing to begin my day. My feet hit the floor as I pushed myself up to start getting ready. However, I noticed I was a little stiff. I had been lying down for several hours, and my body had to readjust. Taking the first step took some energy as my limbs were waking up too. My limbs were responsible for supporting my effort to walk and to move. Without their cooperation, I would not have been able to get out of bed, let alone walk.

Walk is such a simple term and such a simple action, or is it? It can actually have a dual meaning as it describes a form of locomotion but can also refer to a journey or a destination. When we walk, the body (torso) actually vaults over our stiff limbs with each step. In other words, we are literally carrying something as we walk. And in carrying this, we have a destination to get to. Our limbs are challenged every day when we walk because they literally hold up our bodies and bring balance to our movement. Walking in itself has numerous health benefits: it improves stamina and energy; reduces stress and elevates mood; improves confidence, memory skills, and learning ability; and reduces the risk of osteoporosis, hypertension, diabetes, heart disease, and strokes among other things. Walking is imperative for improving health and sustaining it.

Out of all of the chapters in this book, this one has been the most difficult for me to write, and it has created the greatest struggle. I mean, let's be honest: If walking is so simple and easy, why is it so difficult for some people to relearn once something has threatened their ability to walk? Why do some people decide to stop walking? People can't walk when they lose their balance. They stop walking when they enter a dark space because they become fearful of the invisibility that lies ahead. People stop walking because they become lazy and just want to continue to sit where they are. People stop walking because they start to believe that they'll never make it to where they're trying to go. People stop walking because they've lost their zeal and appetite for health. I've realized that walking is not some idle activity. It is an activity with a purpose designed to get you somewhere.

Following Jesus' command to arise or get up, the Bible says that she *immediately* rose and *walked!* She woke up ready—ready to get to her next, to start living her life again, ready to be healthy, ready to be reconnected, and ready to follow what the Lord spoke to her. I'm reminded of a young child who learns to walk on his/her own for the first time and how he/she can't wait to explore his/her surroundings and get into everything. There is such astonishment on the faces of the parents and family members when they witness their child walking for the first time. Yes, the child might fall several times, but if you notice, that child will do everything he/she has to do to get back up and start walking again once he/she has learned how. Other than being fueled by the curiosity of the external world, the child walks because he/she notices the faces and the attention he/she receives from the family members. Innately, the child wants to make these family members proud, so he/she keeps walking.

Sometimes we've been lying down for so long that we have difficulty getting up to walk or we no longer desire to walk. If you're anything like me, you've remained in a sedentary place for too long. Yet something inside of you is squirming in discomfort because it's time to change your posture. Biologically, the body will not take more rest than what it needs. We may sleep for several hours, but when the body has gotten what it needs, the brain alerts the rest of the systems to wake and move. I don't know what has crippled your walk, be it fear, lack of motivation, fatigue, unbelief, illness, or hopelessness. But I declare to you that today is the day you will walk again! Get up!

Prayer

Lord, now is the time, and today is the day that I begin to walk again. I will walk away from the things that have nothing to do with You and anything that holds me back. I must go forward, even if I must do it afraid and even if I fight to push myself every day. I believe that You're with me and You're guiding me. I trust that in every step I take, I'll get stronger and closer to the life You have designed for me. Order my steps so everywhere I go, it will always lead me into deeper intimacy with You. In Jesus' name, amen.

Reflection Question

What am I willing to walk away from so I can walk into deeper intimacy with Christ and renewed purpose?

_____

_____

_____

_____

_____

_____

_____

_____

_____

_____

_____

_____

_____

_____

_____

_____

_____

_____

DAY

22

Age Is More Than a Number

It is not uncommon to hear the expression, "Age ain't nothing but a number." In other words, age should carry no restrictions. This implies that age should not qualify or limit a person from achieving or participating in a particular thing. In some regard, there may be some validity to the expression. But in this case with Jairus' daughter, I'd have to disagree that age is just merely a number. In fact, this account points to the idea that age is much more than a number.

Whenever I read the Bible, I'm inclined to believe that every detail, no matter how big or small, means something. Part of the Bible code is the random mention of something that doesn't seem to flow with the rest of the story, yet it actually does have meaning if you pay attention and do your historical research and read the story in context. I found it interesting that after she walked, the scripture mentions that the girl was 12 years old. This was significant! In my years of study in the seminary, I was privileged to study the Hebrew language and learn the Jewish culture. Thus, I remembered that the age of 12 (or 13 for a boy) was a pivotal point in the life of a Jewish girl and boy. For a girl, she becomes a bat mitzvah, which means "daughter of commandment" and the son becomes bar mitzvah, which means "son of commandment." This coming of age event is typically marked by a ceremony (celebration), yet in the text, we see that it seemed like they were almost gathering for her funeral. She was at an age where she was supposed to be transitioning into adulthood and spiritual maturity, but she was dead! Have you ever been there? You're supposed to be doing certain things and coming into maturity by a certain time, but something killed you.

Jesus knew this! He knew that there was supposed to be a celebration for this little girl and not a funeral. It was her time to transition; it wasn't her time to die! Oh, the irony of this text! He came because death had come upon her, but she wasn't supposed to be dead. Her dreams weren't supposed to be dead, her speech wasn't supposed to be dead, her destiny wasn't supposed to be dead, her relationships weren't supposed to be dead, and nothing connected to her was supposed to be dead. So I say the same thing to you. I don't care how young or old you are. You are not supposed to be dead! You're reading this book because you are transitioning into a greater you and a deeper intimacy with God. Yes, your age means everything! Now get to doing what you're supposed to be doing! Get up!

Prayer

God, give me the grace and the ardent passion to do that which You have chosen me to do in the earth. I shake death off of me now in whatever capacity it tries to attach itself to me. I recommit to doing the work You have assigned to my hands, and I honor You with my age, knowing that I'm not too young and it's never too late. In Jesus' name, amen.

Reflection Question

Regardless of your age, what will you recommit yourself to today?

_____

_____

_____

_____

_____

_____

_____

_____

_____

_____

_____

_____

_____

_____

_____

_____

_____

_____

_____

_____

_____

_____

DAY

23

Rights

In Western culture, we earn specific rights when we reach a particular age. For instance, at the age of 16, we obtain a license for the right to drive; the age of 18 ushers us into adulthood; and at the age of 21 we are considered full, independent adults with the legal right to do what we choose to do. So the same principle existed in Jewish culture. The ages of 12 and 13 for Jewish girls and boys are transitional ages. It is a time when they are celebrated for their entry into adulthood, though they are not considered full-fledged adults yet.

At this age, they are given certain rights under four specific categories: spiritual disciplines, moral and ethical accountability, legal rights, and marital rights. Under spiritual disciplines, the girl or boy gains the right and responsibility of performing certain rituals, leading prayer services, reading from the Torah, fasting, lighting Shabbat candles, and performing acts of charity. In terms of moral and ethical accountability, they are considered able to distinguish between right and wrong and become responsible for their own actions and sins. Legally, they gain the right to own property and/or enter into a contract. And lastly, marital rights allow them to technically be married, but it is recommended for them to marry between ages sixteen to eighteen. So what's happening here is that as she/he is physically maturing (developing), and she/he is simultaneously reaching a moral maturity at the same time. This is what it means to be a son or daughter of commandment.

When you have reached the stage where you look the part and your morals have been activated then, it's *time to live the part!* Once God raises you, there are rights and responsibilities you are expected to carry out. And He gives you the authority to do so. Jairus' daughter rose and entered into the rights and responsibilities that accompanied her age. Today, I make a declaration over you that your rights have been restored! Now carry out your responsibilities of prayer, worship, reading the Word, fasting, repentance, making honorable decisions, claiming territory, and upholding your covenant relationships. Walk in your authority to cast down strongholds, renounce and break demonic agreements, build up and edify the people of God, and declare faith and manifestation. You have been given everything you need for life and godliness. Get up and use it!

Prayer

God, I give You praise for bringing me into a place of maturity, a place where You can trust me to carry out a piece of Your mission. Give me the grace, discipline, and desire to uphold the mandate You have placed over my life and the responsibilities that come with it. I walk in Your authority, knowing that I am a son/daughter of commandment. In Jesus' name, amen.

Reflection Question

What is the mandate God has given you, and what are the associated responsibilities?

_____

_____

_____

_____

_____

_____

_____

_____

_____

_____

_____

_____

_____

_____

_____

_____

_____

_____

_____

DAY

24

Amazement

The word *amazement* in the Greek language and modern-day English carries with it the sense of bewilderment, meaning that one is actually removed from his/her senses and enters into some sort of an ecstatic trance-like state. The language here (whether *amazement* or *astonishment* are used, depending on the translation) is quite strong. It aims to express the intensity of emotional experience felt by the people who witnessed this girl's transformation and resurrection.

I really enjoy watching makeover shows or TV shows like *Say Yes to the Dress* because you get to see ordinary people being made over in extraordinary ways. They often come into the makeover room with signs of stress, overwhelm, and sadness because life has over-taken their sense of worth, strength, and beauty. They are literally just existing but not living at all. It's almost like they're the walking dead. Yet when they get made over, there is a bright, joyful counte-nance that engulfs their faces; a renewed confidence and fierceness finds its way into their stride with every new step they take. And to add to their personal experience, their family members are usually in utter amazement when they see this transformed person. If you notice, the family members become trance-like and will just stare in disbelief and excitement with tears escaping their eyes as if they've just seen a miracle.

I'm sure this is what happened with Jairus' daughter. She was seen sick, then she was seen dead. Now she was seen living without the cloud of sickness and death over her. Isn't that something? What a miracle it is for our souls and spirits to be revived. Think about how much of an impact your revival will make on others who saw you in a sick and deadened state. How excited they will be to see you rise and be who you are! Imagine how awesome it will be to be a greater version of yourself! Well, what are you waiting for? It's time. There are souls assigned to you. People are waiting for you. Get up!

Prayer

Lord, I am still amazed by You. You are the ultimate makeover artist. I pray that those who witnessed my resurrection will experience their own. And we can all stand in awe and amazement at Your power and the works of Your hands. In Jesus' name, amen.

Reflection Question

How do you envision your future? What are things God could do that would be amazing to you?

_____

_____

_____

_____

_____

_____

_____

_____

_____

_____

_____

_____

_____

_____

_____

_____

_____

_____

_____

_____

DAY

25

Shhh, Don't Tell Anyone

I can honestly say that I'm pretty good at keeping secrets. If someone tells me something in confidence, I will never want to violate that person's trust in me. So generally speaking, his/her secret is safe with me unless it involves any kind of intentional harm. However, I must admit that it's harder for me to keep a secret when it's new and exciting news. Sometimes I feel like I'm going to burst wide open if I have to contain something good over some time. But I have to realize two things amid that urge to tell someone: (1) it's likely not my business to tell, and (2) there's a time for this news to be shared and known.

Jesus specifically told the witnesses not to say anything about this girl being resurrected. At first, I was a bit confused by this because I wondered how something this great could happen yet not be shared. Like, why would Jesus not want anyone to know? I mean, weren't they going to find out, anyway? There is no concrete reason in the scriptures that explains why Jesus gave these instructions. However, I'm inclined to believe it has to do with the timing and manifestation. Timing is everything. There are a couple of times in the Gospels when Jesus gave specific instructions for people not to talk about the miracles he had just performed because it wasn't time yet. Some things have to be understood in time. Additionally, manifestation trumps talk any day. In other words, there's no need to tell what happened. Just let people see it.

Everything that God is doing in your life and through you does not always need to be mentioned. Some things are just between you and God. Let Him work on you in secret. Allow Him to groom you by His hands in the closed chamber. And when the timing is right, He'll unveil you to the world. Then they'll see with their own eyes the wondrous things that God has done in and for you, and all glory will be His. Get up!

Prayer

Lord, I thank You for the time You've taken to prepare me in the secret place. I thank You for raising me for more. Help me to learn to keep my mouth shut and allow my existence to testify of Your miraculous power. In Jesus' name, amen.

Reflection Question

What does God say to you in private?

_____

_____

_____

_____

_____

_____

_____

_____

_____

_____

_____

_____

_____

_____

_____

_____

_____

_____

_____

_____

DAY

26

Time To Eat

Growing up in my household, when dinner was ready, my Mom would often yell, "Stacia, time to eat!" I'd go running downstairs, eager to fix my plate because I knew it was going to be something good and also because I was just hungry. Every day, when I came home from school, my Dad would ask, "What did you eat today? Did you eat any vegetables?" My parents were very big on nourishment and nutrition. I grew to develop this habit particularly when I moved out on my own because I often heard their voices in the back of my head, asking me if I had eaten and if I ate my vegetables. It was truly annoying but necessary. I later realized that they were basically holding me accountable for two main things: (1) taking care of myself and (2) making sure I fed myself the right things. My parents were onto something.

There's a science to losing weight and being healthy. The 80–20 rule emphasizes that to lose weight and/or be healthy, 80 percent is what you eat, and 20 percent is exercise. Food, especially the right food, is fuel for the body. Food is what gives the body energy and the strength to keep going. Food is mood; it plays a major role in our emotional wellness. It is what helps heal the body during a period of sickness, and it is what helps the body make a full recovery. Nutrition is essential to our overall health and well-being.

So it's not strange that once Jesus rose Jairus' daughter and she walked, he commanded the people to give her something to eat. What a moment this must've been that Jesus, the Bread of Life, told the people to give her something to eat. Matthew 4:4 says that "man shall not live on bread alone, but by every word that proceeds from the mouth of God." We really see this come to life in this account because she came back to life and literally lived off of a word from Jesus. He Himself fed her spiritually since He was the Living Word. Yet she still needed to be fed naturally because her body was recovering. Jesus was right there to give her what she needed spiritually and to point her in the direction to get what she needed naturally.

Now that you're up and walking, what are you feeding yourself? Are you feasting on the Word of God daily? Are you watching what you put into your body naturally? God is all about wellness and wholeness. We are His temple, and as He breathes into us, we are given a charge to take care of our bodies, souls, and spirits. C'mon, it's time to eat! Get up!

Prayer

God, I admit I have not been the best at taking care of myself and feeding myself the right things. I honor the fact that You have breathed new life into me and caused my spirit to rise again. Help me to consistently feed myself Your Word and feed my body proper nutrients. Increase my appetite for You and the right things. In Jesus' name, amen.

Reflection Question

What do you enjoy about reading the Word of God? What stops you from reading it consistently?

_____

_____

_____

_____

_____

_____

_____

_____

_____

_____

_____

_____

_____

_____

_____

_____

_____

_____

_____

_____

DAY

27

The Comeback

I remember some of the lyrics to a song by LL Cool Jay, a famous hip-hop rap artist, say, "Don't call it a comeback / I been here for years." He was, in effect, sending a message to his critics/opponents that he may have fallen, but he's still here, and he's coming for them. It was what we would call a diss track, and it turned out to be one of the greatest diss tracks of all time both critically and commercially. It was a song of combat. In his lyrics, he referenced shadowboxing. I'm not much of a sports person, so I had to do a little bit of research to see exactly what shadowboxing was. I found it is an exercise used in the training for combat sports, mainly in boxing. Its purpose is to prepare the muscles before the person training engages in stronger physical activity. In shadowboxing, only one person is required to participate, and the boxer throws punches at no one in particular. Apparently, boxing trainers prefer that their fighters do their shadowboxing before engaging in any other daily exercise routine. The main purpose of this exercise, apart from getting the muscles ready for another activity, is usually to maintain a fighter's rhythm and also to show the fighter how he/she will look at that stage of training against a certain opponent. There are even styles of shadowboxing such as the long method and the short method. For instance, the *long* method involves a shuffle of the feet that rocks the body back and forth. This is a popular style used by fighters with a long reach who use more straight shots and jabs. The *short* method sees the fighter move his head and body to the right and the left, constantly slipping punches and moving in for closer body shots. Joe Frazier and Mike Tyson are among the best examples of fighters who used this method. And would you believe that the term *shadowboxing* is also employed in the field of psychology? Psychology refers to shadowboxing as the process of overcoming a negative self-image that could prevent an individual from achieving success.

Nothing is better than a comeback! Being down twenty points in the fourth quarter yet winning the game, graduating from school when people told you you'd never make it, coming back to life when the doctors said you would not live, and emerging as a confident person who once detested what you saw in the mirror are all examples of a comeback. It's important to realize that there was a great you before you got to a low point, and there's a greater you that will emerge from this point moving forward. Jairus' daughter was one of the biblical models of a comeback. Because of Jesus, her comeback game was strong! She basically sent a message to her sickness and her opponent, death, that "you will not win, you will not hold me down any longer, and I'm coming back to show you that I'm here."

It's time for the comeback in your life. Start training those muscles again, check out how you look in this new place, and enhance the way you look at yourself. Go hard, and be authentically you! Your enemy ain't got nothing on you! Get up!

Prayer

Lord, You are the King of the comeback and the most renowned trainer of all times. Praise be to You, the Lord, my Rock, who trains my hands for war and my fingers to fight. Give me the strength and strategy to come back for everything that's mine. In Jesus' name, amen.

Reflection Question

Who were you before the comeback, and who will you be after the comeback?

_____

_____

_____

_____

_____

_____

_____

_____

_____

_____

_____

_____

_____

_____

_____

_____

_____

_____

DAY

28

Be You

A long time ago, my Mom told me the story about when she first realized she was pregnant with me. The most interesting thing about the story was that her doctor kept telling her that she was not pregnant! According to his medical opinion, there was no evidence of a baby. Yet somehow my Mom knew I was there. She sensed me, she felt differently, and she knew something had happened that was not characteristic of her. Obviously, at some point I was made known, and the doctor confirmed her pregnancy. I was an underdog from the beginning and often went undetected on the radar of most people. This would be the backdrop of my life.

From the time that I was a little girl, I was fully aware that I was quite different. I thought differently and acted differently. I just felt weird. Well into my teen years, I felt like I never fit in and was often rejected. My college years were the first time in my life I had ever felt truly embraced by my peers and found people I could really connect to, and I still have many of those connections to this day. What I had to learn was my uniqueness and being okay in it.

We are never meant to be someone else. Sometimes we can work so hard at being carbon copies of a portion of someone else's life that we become completely clueless about how to be authentically ourselves! Jairus' daughter was clearly unique, and if she wasn't unique in the people's eyes before Jesus raised her, she was definitely unique afterward! There was no way that she was going to be like anyone else after this ordeal. She couldn't. Neither can you. God has resurrected someone amazing. He's given you words of life, He's given you influence, He's given you vision, and He's given you a specific place in the world to impact. Not being you will dishonor God, and it will be a tragedy to those He assigned to you. Let God show you who you are, and *be* that! You may fly under the people's radar, but God knows your name and He will cause the right people to discern your presence and help you to be who He has designed you to be with confidence and with a full appreciation of who you are. Get up!

Prayer

Lord, being me is not always easy, and it doesn't always feel comfortable. But this is who I am. Empower me to be the best me I can ever be. Thank You for being the God who sees me. The best way I can honor You is to be the exact product You have manufactured me to be. I recommit to honoring You with my authenticity. Please help me to give You full access to draw it out. In Jesus' name, amen.

Reflection Question

What are some of the great, fun, quirky, annoying things and qualities that make you, you?

_____

_____

_____

_____

_____

_____

_____

_____

_____

_____

_____

_____

_____

_____

_____

_____

_____

DAY

29

Hope

This morning, I woke up to the sound of birds chirping outside my window. They're normally there every morning, but for some reason they were extra loud today. Instead of being annoyed, I smiled and thanked God because they served as a reminder that there's something beautiful awaiting me outside: life! And regardless of what is happening, life is something I'm excited to live because I believe I'm going to see and experience amazing things. Essentially, *hope* is about an expectation or having a desire for something. When we hope for something, we look forward to its manifestation and fulfillment. In other words, we want something to happen or be true.

One thing that I admire about Jairus is the fact that he didn't lose his hope, even though the situation warranted that. He could have thrown everything away once he found out his daughter was actually dead. I mean, think about it: Who runs for help after someone has died? We usually accept reality as the truth. Not Jairus. I believe he saw more for his daughter, and he was convinced that there was supposed to be more to her life. Somewhere in his mind, he refused to accept that things were actually supposed to be this way. So he sought out Jesus because that was his last hope and his greatest hope. With his own eyes, he watched his hope manifest in the resurrection of his daughter.

Regardless of what you see or where you find yourself, there is hope for you. There is hope for your dreams, your ministry, your business, your health, your mental stability, your children, and your marriage. If you're in a place now where life has been unkind and you've lost all hope, I speak new hope back into your spirit. You are a raised son and a raised daughter; therefore, there is no other expectation than for you to live a life, hoping forward and full of expectation. Be the embodiment of hope. There are people around you who need to see that. Get up!

Prayer

God, I stand in a resurrected place that is built on Your promises. You alone are my hope, and it is in You that I place my trust. In the face of what can sometimes look like hopelessness and uncertainty, I declare manifestation, fulfillment, peace, excitement, and renewed purpose. I walk in it in Jesus' name. Amen.

Reflection Question

What are the declarations of hope that you can speak over your life?

_____

_____

_____

_____

_____

_____

_____

_____

_____

_____

_____

_____

_____

_____

_____

_____

_____

DAY

30

A Resurrected Praise

Wow! What a journey back to life! To go from a sickness that escalates to a death experience that ultimately culminates in a resurrection and restored life is noteworthy of praise! What is there left to give? I sit and imagine what the atmosphere must've been like immediately, following the resurrection and restoration of Jairus' daughter. No one can tell me that there wasn't praise! How could there not be? Look at what Jesus did! A girl became sick and died at the moment of her transition, at a time where she was supposed to be celebrating her coming of age, yet Jesus gave her back her life. He gave her reasons to live again. She had stuff to do! And so do you!

I've learned several things about praise. It is an antidote for depression and anxiety. During praise, worship, and prayer are the only times your brain/nervous system is equally aroused and relaxed at the same time, producing a feeling of unity and communion with God. One of my favorite things about praise is that it speaks my enemy's destruction and his defeat. I mock my enemy in praise, letting him know that he couldn't kill me or keep me down. In praise, I speak the language of my God. I shift myself in the spirit. I realign myself with my God and with my true self. And in response, God sends ambushments in the spirit realm.

You have survived! You've come through sickness and death. Death cannot hold you. You have defeated death and come back to life. You owe God praise just for that! So gather your instruments, use your limbs to lift and clap, use your feet to dance, open your mouth, and make a sound unto your God! Come on, you can do it! You've been resurrected, and you've crossed over, so here's to new life. Welcome back! Welcome to your next. He got up so you can *Get up*!

Prayer

Lord, I give You praise for seeing me through this journey. It wasn't easy, but it was what I needed to take my life back. I praise You now for deeper intimacy; restoration; new strategies; improved well-being; increased wealth, covenant relationships, effective ministry, and business models; and a stronger, more empowered me. Help me to maintain this posture so I shall not die but live to declare the works of the Lord. In Jesus' name, amen!

Reflection Question

What does praise mean to you, and how will you praise God now?

_____

_____

_____

_____

_____

_____

_____

_____

_____

_____

_____

_____

_____

_____

_____

_____

_____

_____

_____

_____

_____

EPILOGUE
FOR HIM

This has been life-changing for me, and I hope and pray you will have the same sentiment after taking this journey. What I have realized is that this is, in fact, a journey that doesn't end. It's just a blueprint. Why? Because we will constantly be challenging ourselves to get up from things that make us sick or threaten to kill us and blow out the candle on our relationship with Christ. But we must remember who we are and whose we are to live resurrected lives.

For me, I know I almost don't have a choice. You see, my name actually comes from the Greek name *Anastasis*, which means "resurrection, rising, or rebirth." It also means "recovery from a debilitating condition." So every time someone says my name, he/she doesn't even realize the fact that they're speaking life to me. Every time they call my name, they are telling me to get up, recover, and come back to life. God named me in His image and filled me with His Spirit so I can't die. Death is not who I am! In biblical times, a name had meaning and served as a person's reputation. My reputation is not one of death but one of life, one who recovers when she is knocked down. And trust me, I've been through a lot that was designed to kill me, but I always came back. It's because of who He is and what He calls me.

God is beyond amazing! He has a way of speaking over your life before you even know who He is and who you are. He's constantly revealing the depths of Himself, and He just wants us to take ahold of it. We weren't created for ourselves. We were created for Him. So it's always about Him. After preaching and teaching this sermon in various renditions and now writing this book, He's still revealing Himself. And the greatest thing that I have realized through His revelation as I come to the end of this book is the fact that Jairus' daughter rose for Him (Jesus). I remembered a little about the Hebrew language after studying it some years ago, and I knew that *cum* (*koum*) meant "to arise or get up." But I realized that the scripture says "*cumi*." I thought that had to be plural for something, or there was something more to that command than what I thought I knew. What I found was mind-blowing! When Jesus said, "*Talitha, cumi*," to Jairus' daughter, he wasn't just telling her to get up. He was saying, "Little girl, get up *for me*." How intimate is that! Our hearts melt when we ask someone for a favor, and then we say, "Do it for me," and then the person actually does it. That's love, that's respect, and that's value.

So even when you don't feel like doing certain things or you'd rather remain in negative emotions, remember that God is asking you to get up for Him. Don't do it for you; do it for Him. Only what we do for Christ will last. We owe Him our lives, and if He brings us out of anything alive, it is our responsibility to live for Him. The time has come, and He has need of you. *Get Up, For Him!*

ABOUT THE AUTHOR

Dr. Stacia (affectionately known as Dr. Stay) has worked as a professionally trained psychotherapist for over 15 years with a variety of populations in diverse settings yet specializing in the psychospiritual care of survivors of abusive relationships and organizational systems. She is a passionate speaker who has facilitated several conferences/ workshops surrounding male and female issues, mental health and self-care, spiritual growth, and leadership development. She operates from a psychospiritual wellness model that teaches individuals, teams, and organizations how to recognize the historical underpinnings that have shaped unhealthy internal cultures, reframe cognitive constructs, revitalize emotional health, and restore broken barriers to safe environments by using practical methods to help others return to a state of wellness and proficiency.

Dr. Stacia is the Founder and Chief Visionary Officer (CVO) of Darar Enterprises, LLC, which is the parent company of two subsidiaries: Heart 4 Christ Ministries and SKW Counseling & Consulting. She is a state Licensed Professional Counselor with a Bachelor's degree in Psychology from Delaware State University (Dover, Delaware), a Master's degree in Mental Health Counseling from the Alliance Graduate School of Counseling (Nyack, New York), a Master's degree in Divinity from the Alliance Theological Seminary (Nyack, New York), and a Doctorate in Clinical Psychology from California Southern University (Costa Mesa, California). Dr. Stacia is a native of Wilmington, Delaware, and currently resides in Pennsylvania with her loving husband, Andre Wilkins.

Facebook: Dr.Stay
Instagram: iamdrstay
Website: www.dararenterprises.org